The Life and Work of...
HENRY MOORE

Sean Connolly

Heinemann
LIBRARY

www.heinemann.co.uk
Visit our website to find out more information about Heinemann Library books.

To order:

☎ Phone 44 (0) 1865 888066

▤ Send a fax to 44 (0) 1865 314091

▤ Visit the Heinemann Bookshop at www.heinemann.co.uk to browse our catalogue and order online.

First published in Great Britain by Heinemann Library, Halley Court, Jordan Hill, Oxford OX2 8EJ, a division of Reed Educational and Professional Publishing Ltd.
Heinemann is a registered trademark of Reed Educational and Professional Publishing Ltd.

OXFORD MELBOURNE AUCKLAND JOHANNESBURG BLANTYRE
GABORONE IBADAN PORTSMOUTH (NH) USA CHICAGO

© Reed Educational and Professional Publishing Ltd 2001

Designed by Celia Floyd
Originated by Dot Grdations   Printed by South China Printing in Hong Kong/China

ISBN 0 431 13151 1 (hardback)   ISBN 0 431 13156 2 (paperback)
05 04 03 02 01   05 04 03 02 01
10 9 8 7 6 5 4 3 2 1   10 9 8 7 6 5 4 3 2 1

British Library Cataloguing in Publication Data

Connolly, Sean
 The life and work of Henry Moore. – (Take-off!)
 1.Moore, Henry, 1898–1986 – Juvenile literature
 2.Sculptors – England – Biography – Juvenile literature
 3.Sculpture, Modern – 20th century – England – Juvenile literature
 I.Title II.Henry Moore
 730.9'2

Acknowledgements

The publishers would like to thank the following for permission to reproduce photographs: The Henry Moore Foundation for: Page 4, Portrait studio, 1960. Page 5, Henry Moore 'Three Forms: Vertebrae'. Page 6, Henry Moore aged 11. Page 7, Castleford Grammar School's Roll of Honour. Page 8, Henry Moore convalescing at Castleford Grammar School 1918. Page 9, Henry Moore 'Small Animal Head 1921'. Page 10, Corner of studio, Adie Road 1928. Page 11, Henry Moore 'Reclining Figure 1929'. Page 12, Henry Moore with 'West Wind' 1928. Page 13, North wall of Headquarters of London Underground. Page 14, Corner of studio at 11a Parkhill Road, Hampstead 1936. Page 15, Henry Moore 'Reclining Figure 1936'. Page 17, Henry Moore 'Two forms 1934'. Page 18, Lee Miller, Henry Moore in Holborn Underground, London 1943. Page 19, Henry Moore 'Pink and Green Sleepers 1941'. Page 20, Lee Miller Archives, Henry Moore with Severini in Venice for the Biennale 1948. Page 21, Henry Moore 'Madonna and Child'. Page 22, Henry Moore carving UNESCO 'Reclining Figure 1957-58'. Page 23 Henry Moore 'Draped Reclining Figure 1952-53'. Page 24, Henry Moore in top studio 1954. Page 25, Henry Moore 'Double Oval'. Page 26, Henry Moore working in new maquette studio 1978. Page 27, Henry Moore 'Sheep Piece 1962-63'. Page 28, The *Independent*. Page 29, Henry Moore 'Large Figure in a Shelter 1952-53'. Page 16, Robert Harding Picture Library

Cover photograph reproduced with permission of the Henry Moore Foundation.

Contents

Any words appearing in the text in bold,
like this, are explained in the Glossary.

Who was Henry Moore?

Henry Moore was one of the most important artists of this century. He made huge **sculptures** out of stone, wood and **bronze**. He also made many drawings.

This photograph of Henry Moore was taken in 1960.

People from around the world asked Henry Moore to make sculptures for them. This sculpture stands in Dallas, Texas, USA.

Henry Moore made this sculpture in 1978.

sculpture

Henry Moore made about 800 sculptures in wood, bronze and stone.

Early years

Henry Moore was born on 30 July 1898 in Castleford, England. His father was a miner. When Henry was 12 years old he won a **scholarship** to Castleford Secondary School.

A photograph of Henry when he was 11 years old.

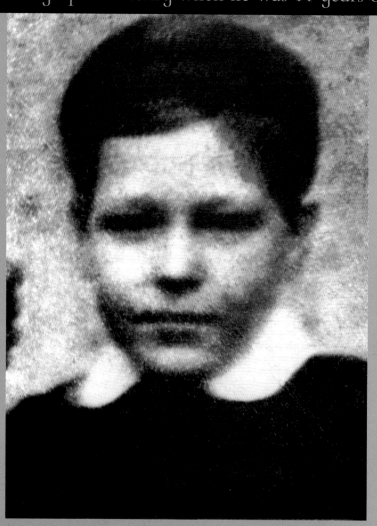

Henry was already good at art. When he was 16 years old, his teachers asked him to **carve** this **roll of honour** for the school.

The roll of honour which Henry's teachers asked him to carve. It lists the names of the former pupils of the school who died in the First World War.

The **First World War** lasted from 1914 to 1918.

London

Henry fought in the **First World War** for two years. In 1921 he began studying at the Royal College of Art in London. Two years later he visited Paris.

This photograph of Henry was taken in 1918.

Henry joined the army when he was 17 years old. He was the youngest member of his regiment.

Henry saw many types of art in London and Paris.

A **sculpture** of a small animal head that Henry made in London in 1921.

Settling in

In 1924 Moore became a teacher at the Royal College of Art in London. He was also busy making his own **sculptures**. In 1928 he had a one-man **exhibition** in London.

A photograph of a corner of Moore's studio.

Moore **carved** his sculptures out of stone or wood. He liked to show people **reclining**. He made many more sculptures like this one.

Moore made this sculpture called *Reclining Figure* in 1929.

Moore made lots of sculptures of women reclining. They often seem to be looking into the distance.

The public eye

Moore working on his first commission.

Moore became more famous. When he was 31 he did his first **commission**. It was a huge **sculpture** for the London Underground.

The sculpture called *West Wind*.

The title of this sculpture is *West Wind*. Moore was interested in stone, fire, water and wind.

The sculpture can be seen on the wall of the headquarters of London Underground.

The modern world

In the 1930s Moore became interested in **abstract** art. His **sculpture** began to look less like human beings and more like simple, rounded shapes.

The rounded shapes of Henry's abstract sculptures.

Moore collected pebbles, stones and shells to see how nature creates shapes. This statue shows Moore's interest in smooth, curved surfaces.

One of Moore's statues with smooth surfaces.

Getting known

More and more people saw the beauty in Moore's large **sculptures**. They were **exhibited** in Europe and the USA.

This is a picture of the Museum of Modern Art in New York, USA.

This sculpture is called *Two Forms*.

Moore sold this sculpture to the Museum of Modern Art in New York, USA, in 1934. It shows how his sculptures at this time were only partly **abstract**. Many people see human shapes in this sculpture.

17

War artist

The **Second World War** began in 1939. Two years later Moore was asked to become an official war artist. He drew the daily life of people in London during the war.

Moore drawing people trying to sleep in the underground.

These drawings are some of Moore's most powerful works. This one shows people trying to sleep while bombs explode outside.

The crayon marks in Moore's drawings look like the chisel marks on a stone sculpture.

Travelling the world

After the war Moore travelled to many places. He got many prizes for his sculptures.

Henry Moore and a friend in Venice, Italy.

Moore's prizes did not change the look of his sculptures. He made this **tender** sculpture of Mary and Jesus for a church in Suffolk.

This sculpture is called *Madonna and Child.*

Time for a change

In the 1950s Moore tried new ways of working. Until then he carved directly from blocks of stone or wood. Now he made many **sculptures** from **bronze**.

Moore working on a sculpture.

This bronze sculpture of a woman is in front of a building in London.

Moore could make even bigger, smoother
sculptures out of bronze.

Moore shaped most of his large works as small clay
models first. Then he made big versions of them in bronze.

New ideas

Henry also looked for new ideas. In the 1950s he began putting one shape inside another one.

Moore with a sculpture with shapes going inside others.

sculptures

If you walk around these sculptures, you see how different they are.

Moore wanted people to look at his large **sculptures** from all sides. These two sculptures seem alike at first. They only look different when you walk around them.

Once, when Moore was asked to make a sculpture for a town square, he was asked not to leave any holes where children could get their heads stuck!

The sculptor's studio

Henry Moore working in Perry Green.

Moore moved to Perry Green in Hertfordshire when London was bombed during the war. He was very happy there.

This picture of Moore was taken in 1978. How old was he?

Sheep **grazed** in the field outside Moore's **studio**. In the 1970s Moore made many sketches of the sheep. He made this **sculpture** to go in the field.

This sculpture is called *Sheep Pieces*.

sculpture

An active life ends

Moore still worked when he was more than 80 years old. A special service was held in Westminster Abbey honoured him after his death on 31 August 1986.

A newspaper clipping showing Moore friends arriving at Westminster Abbey.

Mourning Henry Moore yesterday: Jeremy Thorpe; Lord Snowdon and Sir Hugh Casson; Moore's daughter Mary Danowski and her children; Michael Foot and his wife, Jill Craigie.

Friends pay tribute to Moore

FELLOW ARTISTS and friends of the sculptor Henry Moore paid their last respects at a memorial service in Westminster Abbey yesterday. Many of his surviving contemporaries including his widow, Irina, whom he married in 1929, were too frail to attend.

Sir Stephen Spender, the poet, told the congregation that Moore, who died in August, aged 88, was the seventh son of a Yorkshire miner who never considered anyone either socially superior or inferior to himself.

Sir Stephen, one of the last surviving members of Moore's avant-garde Hamp-

stead artistic circle in the Thirties, delivered the address in a brisk, husky whisper. He remembered Moore's studio as a focal point for artists, including Ben Nicholson, the painter, and Barbara Hepworth, the sculptress.

He said that despite Moore's admiration for the abstract artists around him, "he told me he could never make an artefact which referred to nothing but itself".

Moore had confided to him: "Try as I

might, my work always ended up looking like something, probably a reclining figure."

Sir Stephen quoted Sir Herbert Read, the poet and art critic, and a champion of Moore in the Thirties, saying that in his opinion the sculptor would have been the best possible ambassador from this planet to another.

Sir Stephen said: "He was an artist of great ingenuity and a man of great

humanity." Moore had never forgotten the simplicity of his upbringing.

Dame Peggy Ashcroft, the actress, read the first lesson, not from the Bible but from the Apocrypha, the second book of Esdras. It concluded: "He who made all things, and searcheth out hidden things in hidden places, surely he knoweth your imagination, and what ye think in your hearts." The text was suggested to the Moore family by Westminster Abbey, be-

cause its words were so appropriate.

The second lesson, read by the Duke of Gloucester, was from Revelations, in the King James version, chosen because it is the one familiar to Moore's generation.

The congregation included the Prime Minister; Michael Foot, the former Labour leader; Sir Hugh Casson, the architect and painter; Sir Roy Strong, director of the Victoria and Albert Museum; Jeremy Thorpe, the former Liberal leader; John Profumo, the former Conservative Cabinet minister, Lord Snowdon and Sam Wanamaker, the film maker.

List of mourners, page 13

Moore made this **bronze sculpture** just one year before he died.

Read this page carefully. Then use the timeline to work out when Moore made this sculpture.

This is the largest bronze work that Moore ever made.

Timeline

1898	Henry Moore is born in Castleford, Yorkshire on 30 July.
1906	The artist Paul Cézanne dies.
1910	Henry enters Castleford Grammar School on a **scholarship**.
1912	The passenger ship *Titanic* sinks.
1914–18	The **First World War** is fought.
1917	Henry joins the Army and fights in the First World War.
1921	Henry enters the Royal College of Art, London, on a scholarship.
1924	Henry Moore's first **sculptures** are shown in London.
1926	The artists Claude Monet and Mary Cassatt die.
1928	Moore's first one-man **exhibition** in London.
1929	Moore marries Irina Radestsky and completes major work for London Underground.
1938	Moore takes part in the International Exhibition of **Abstract Art** in the Netherlands.
1939–45	The **Second World War** is fought.
1940	The artist Paul Klee dies.
1941	Moore is made an Official War Artist.
1940s	Moore has exhibitions in USA, Australia, Belgium and other countries.
1948	Moore wins International Prize for Sculpture in Venice.
1955	Moore is made a Companion of Honour in Great Britain.
1969	Neil Armstrong becomes the first person to walk on the Moon.
1977	Henry Moore Foundation begins work in Much Hadham, England.
1986	Henry Moore dies in Perry Green, Hertfordshire on 31 August.

Glossary

abstract art   art that tries to show ideas rather than the way things look

bronze   type of metal

carve   cut into a shape

commission   being asked to make a piece of art

exhibition   public showing of art

First World War   the war in Europe that lasted from 1914 to 1918

graze   wander across a field eating grass

hollow   having an empty inside

miner   someone who works underground to dig for coal

reclining   lying down or leaning

roll of honour   list of names of people who have fought in a war

scholarship   money to pay for school

sculpture   piece of 3-dimensional art made out of stone, wood or other materials

Second World War   the war that was fought in Europe, Africa and Asia from 1939 to 1945

studio   room or building where an artist works

tender   showing kindness and gentleness

Westminster Abbey   an important church in London where services are held for special people

More books to read

The History of Western Sculpture: A Young Person's Guide, Juliet Hestlewood, Belitha Press

More sculptures by Henry Moore to see

Large Reclining Figure, The Henry Moore Foundation, Perry Green, Herts

Two Piece Reclining Figure: Points, The Henry Moore Foundation, Perry Green, Herts

Mask, Tate Britain, London

a b c d e f g h i j k l m n o p q r s t u v w x y z

Index

Titles in the *Life and Work of ...* series include:

Hardback   0 431 13150 3

Hardback   0 431 13153 8

Hardback   0 431 13151 1

Hardback   0 431 13152 X

Find out about the other titles in this series on our website www.heinemann.co.uk/library